AF073294

Red Ted at the beach

Written by Geraldine Kaye

Illustrated by Jan Brychta

Lucy had a red bear.
He was called Red Ted.
One day Mum, Dad, Lucy and Sam went to the seaside.

'We can play in the rock pool,' said Lucy.
Lucy put Red Ted on a rock.

A dog saw Red Ted.
He got Red Ted and he ran off.

Mum saw the dog.

She got Red Ted.

'Put Red Ted up here,' said Dad.

Red Ted was on the rock.
A seagull went down and got Red Ted.

The seagull went up and up.
It went up to a nest.
It put Red Ted in the nest.

But the chicks did not like Red Ted.
The seagull got Red Ted out of
the nest.

The seagull went down and down.
It went down to the sea.

Red Ted fell into the sea.

'Oh no!' said Sam.

'Get Red Ted out of the sea!'

Lucy got Red Ted out.
'You can't play in the sea,'
she said.

'You can play here,' said Lucy.